TWO OF EVERYTHING

ADVENTURES OF GRAYSON & AUSTIN

By

Janae Knox

Ilustrations by Tuly Akter

Dedicated to
Grayson, Austin
& Savannah

This book belongs to:

Although we don't live together,
on each other we still rely.

Two pets, two beds, two closets filled with clothes.

We get Two of Everything,
because we have two homes.

The best part about it is
that we've got two rooms.

One decorated with super heroes,
the other stars and moons.

Whether an Astronaut, Doctor, President or head of the marching band.

Our parents tell us anything we want to be we certainly can.

They both make sure we work hard,
winter, spring, summer and fall.

And when we aren't studying or doing schoolwork, we practice basketball.

At our games, both mom and dad cheer us on from the stands.

It's not always easy, but nothing worth having ever is.

You should know that love isn't based on where a person lives.

We are family, we're not perfect,
but still a work of art.

Our love for each other will never change, no matter how far apart.

Holiday's we come together to eat, laugh and love.

And give thanks for our blessings to the sky up above.

Like on Christmas, when we decorate the tree and sing.

And it's our favorite holiday,
because we get Two of Everything.

Acknowledgements

On the nights I was not feeling my best, the days I felt I was not enough, the moments I didn't feel beautiful, there were two little voices that carried me through.

Thank You for inspiring me each and every day. Love Mom.

THE END

Printed in Great Britain
by Amazon

79002797R20016